THUNDERBIRD

THE HIGH-FLYING FORD

by
LINDA CRAVEN
and
JERRY CRAVEN

THE ROURKE CORPORATION, INC.
Vero Beach, FL 32964

ACKNOWLEDGMENTS

We are grateful to Ford Motor Company for supplying the photographs for this book. Special thanks to Carla Banks and Sandra Nicholls for their invaluable assistance.

Library of Congress Cataloging-in-Publication Data

Craven, Linda
    Thunderbird: the high-flying Ford / by Linda Craven and Jerry Craven.
       p. cm. – (Car classics)
    Includes index.
    Summary: Gives a brief history of the Thunderbird automobile describing its special features and most popular models.
    ISBN 0-86593-254-9
    1. Thunderbird automobile – Juvenile literature.
[1. Thunderbird automobile.] I. Craven, Jerry. II. Title.
III. Series: Car classics (Vero Beach, Fla.)
TL215.T46C73 1993
629.222'2 – dc20   93-219
                                            CIP
                                            AC

CONTENTS

CHAPTER 1

IS IT A SPORTS CAR?

When the sassy little Thunderbird made its debut on October 22, 1954, it was a new concept in motoring. While it had the speed and power of a sports car, it also had luxuries not included on other sports cars. For example, it had roll-up side windows, an adjustable steering column and six-way power seats.

Ford officials took a close look, in 1952, at what the American public wanted. They found that there were many sports car clubs, but few owners actually raced their cars.

The 1955 Thunderbird featured slick, straight lines rather than muscle bulges on the hood and fenders, so popular in other sports cars.

Also, Ford learned from their market research that two cars, MG and Jaguar, were the most popular with American sports car drivers. There was, however, a problem. Most MG owners hoped to trade up to a better car as soon as they could. Jaguar was more prestigious, but few could afford it.

Ford researchers decided to build a car that would fit in between MG and Jaguar in price. They wanted the car to be most like the British Jaguar in prestige, size and performance.

Ford officials said the Thunderbird was not a sports car. Instead, they said, it was a "personal car" designed not only for speed and sportiness, but also for comfort and convenience. The public, however, called the first Thunderbird a sports car.

The 1957 Thunderbird was the last of the early 'Birds small enough to be classified a sports car. In 1958 the T-Bird grew into a sedan.

CHAPTER 2

FIRST 'BIRDS

When the 1955 Thunderbird came out, it was an immediate hit with the American public.

Ford first revealed its plans for building a small, fast car at the Detroit Auto Show in February, 1954. The prototype that was uncovered at the show was a wooden mock-up. Some of its design features, such as wheel covers and headlight trim, weren't yet in their final form.

The first 'Birds off the production line appeared in October, 1954. Only the earliest of these '55 models were fitted with Fairlane-style chrome headlight trim and with plain fender skirts. The remainder of the '55 models had plain headlight trim and chrome gravel shields on the fender skirts just like the '56 models.

This 1956 T-Bird offers more trunk space because of the external, continental-style spare tire.

People admired the dashboard of the 1955 Thunderbird for its simplicity and beauty.

Two major changes in body design appeared on the 1956 models. Some drivers complained it was difficult to see in back of the T-Bird through the sides when the removable top was in place. Designers suggested a solution that had been used in the formal coachwork of an earlier era, the now-famous circular window.

To improve ventilation, pop-out cowl vents were also added up front.

To provide more trunk space in the sleek little 'Bird, designers also added an external chamber for the spare tire. A heavy-duty bumper bar wrapped around the spare. The exhaust tips were moved to the outer corners of the bumper, a style that was later used on the Ford Fairlane as well.

CHAPTER 3

WHOSE IDEA? TWO STORIES

Whose idea was it that the Ford Motor Company should build a sports car? There are two stories about how the idea developed.

One story has it that Ford executive Lewis Crusoe visited a Paris auto show in October of 1951. He was impressed by British and European roadsters such as Jaguars, Bugattis and Pegasos. He sent word back to Ford designers telling them to go to work immediately on a sports car design.

The rear fender skirts and the wide white wall tires on this 1955 T-Bird are in keeping with the tastes of the times.

The base price for the 1955 Thunderbird was just $2,695.

According to another account, the idea of a Ford-produced sports car began with auto body designer Franklin Hershey. Before coming to work for Ford, Hershey had custom designed bodies for other famous cars such as Mercedes, Minervas, Cords and Duesenbergs.

Hershey learned from a friend that General Motors Corporation was in the process of designing and building a sports car – the Corvette. So he began designing a competitor that became the Thunderbird.

Perhaps both men came up with the idea. Also, it's certain that both were right – Americans were ready for a small car with classy lines and the ability to fly like the wind.

So the Ford Motor Company produced a car that would become one of the most popular in the country – the Thunderbird.

CHAPTER 4

WHAT'S IN A NAME?

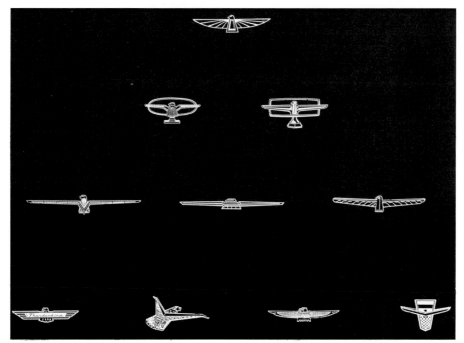

These are some of the emblems used on classic Thunderbirds.

A hot little Ford had been conceived, and a prototype had been displayed at the 1954 Detroit Auto Show. There was not yet a name for the classy new baby.

An advertising agency suggested several, including: Hep Cat, Fordette, Fordster, Beaver, Detroiter, Flag Liner and Wheelaway. One Ford executive, Lewis Crusoe, suggested Savile and offered an expensive new suit of clothes to anyone who could do better.

Ford stylist Alden R. "Gib" Giberson came up with the name *Thunderbird. Bird* suggested flight and speed, and *thunder* suggested power and drama.

In Native American lore, the thunderbird was a powerful spirit in the form of a beautiful bird. Lightning flashed from its beak, and thunder rolled at the beating of its wings. It brought the rain that watered the earth and caused life-giving plants to grow.

The thunderbird fit the image Ford wanted for the sleek, powerful new car. So Thunderbird it became.

The 1993 T-Bird has the latest emblem in the center of the steering wheel.

This is the 35th anniversary model T-Bird. It came out in 1990 and featured a special enamel-on-metal Thunderbird emblem.

Over the years, a number of different emblem designs have graced the Thunderbird bodies. When designers change the look of the car for a new model, they like to create a new version for the emblem that represents Thunderbird.Thunderbird's 35th anniversary in 1990 was celebrated with a new emblem made with cloisonné. Cloisonné is an ancient and beautiful process of baking enamel on metal. It is usually used for jewelry or art objects.

One unique feature of the anniversary emblem is that it shatters if anyone tries to remove it; this prevents its being placed on another model.

CHAPTER 5

FAST 'BIRDS

The original 1955 Thunderbird amazed those who first put it through road tests. Race driver Jack McAfee took the 'Bird from 0 to 60 mph in just 9.5 seconds. He travelled a quarter mile in 16.9 seconds – an impressive record for 1955.

Car magazine writers praised the Thunderbird as a new concept in autos. The amazing thing was that it had sports car qualities – speed and power – yet it had the riding comfort of larger luxury cars.

At the Daytona Speed Weeks, a 1955 'Bird clocked in at 124.633 mph. It beat all other cars there except a Jaguar XK-120-M.

The hard top on this 1956 model was designed to be removed and replaced with ease. The car was called a "hard-top convertible."

1955 Thunderbird

Engine
    Overhead valve V-8
    292 cubic inches
Manual transmission
    8.1:1 compression ratio
    190 brake horse power (bhp)
Automatic transmission
    8.5:1 compression ratio
    198 bhp

In 1956 famous driver Peter De Paolo accelerated a T-Bird from 0 to 88.779 mph in one mile. While not a record, it was excellent performance for any car in 1956.

France was a popular place for sports car races, but many of the roads were poor quality. Nevertheless, the February 10, 1956 *Autocar* magazine raved about the Thunderbird's ability to maintain a comfortable and stable 90-to-100 mph cruising speed on the uneven French roads. Most European sports cars couldn't match that kind of cruising speed.

The super-charged 1957 models had a single four-barrel carburetor and 8.5:1 compression ratio. The 312 cubic inch V-8 was rated at 300 brake horsepower (bhp). One driver clocked his supercharger at an unofficial 0 to 60 mph in 5.5 seconds. At Daytona a supercharged 'Bird with manual transmission scored 93.312 mph in the Production Sports Car standing-start mile.

The 1993 Thunderbird
offers a range of powerful engines, including
the V-6 with 140 horsepower, the supercharged V-6 with
210 hp, and the V-8 with 200 hp.

CHAPTER 6

RARE 'BIRDS

Car enthusiasts have always loved limited editions, or specialty models produced in limited numbers, making the cars rare.

The "Princess Grace Thunderbird" was just such a limited edition. Only 2,000 of the 1963 Thunderbird Landau were produced. The elegant model was introduced in Monaco by Princess Grace, an American movie star who had married a prince and become a princess.

The white "Princess Grace" T-Birds had white leather upholstery, rosewoodlike trim on dash and console, and a rose vinyl top.

The 1962 Thunderbird sports roadster brought back the two-seater style of earlier 'Birds. The four-seater design was transformed into a two-seater by bolting a fiberglass cover over the back seat.

Writers for *Car Life* magazine said of the stylish '62 roadster, "On the highway it's quiet and smooth, in front of your house it will turn your neighbors green with envy."

In spite of its style and grace, only 1,427 of the '62 sports roadsters were sold.

Even more rare are the 1957 supercharged 'Birds. Only 194 were built with the special centrifugal supercharger. They were known as F-Birds because of the special prefix on their serial numbers.

Fourteen more supercharged 'Birds were built with manual transmissions. They were given serial numbers with the prefix D, so they're sometimes called the D-Birds.

Today, all of the small-production T-Birds are worth far more than the original purchase price.

Both hardtop and convertible Thunderbirds were popular in 1957.

Only 14,912 1956
Thunderbirds were sold.

CHAPTER 7

ALMOST 'BIRDS

The Thunderbird has changed in appearance over the years, as styles have come and gone. Many designs never made it to the showroom floor.

After designer Hershey finished the basic design for the original T-Bird in August of 1954, he went on vacation. Another Ford executive came to see the prototype and made some changes. He included variations of the V-shaped molding on the side, similar to the molding on the 1955 Ford Fairlane. When Hershey returned he was furious. He went straight to Henry Ford II, who ordered the molding removed.

One of the most surprising proposals, given the sporty image of the T-Bird, was for a station wagon model in 1958. The model was never built.

One design that Elwood Engel proposed for the 1961 'Bird became the inspiration for the Lincoln Continental body. Another proposed T-Bird design suggested the later Mustang grille opening.

This 1963 T-Bird was a popular sports roadster.

For the 1962 Thunderbird, designers chose an unbroken line from front to back.

Other proposed designs for the '61 model included a long-finned style, something like the tail-finned Cadillacs of the era. The final production model for the year did have a rocketlike appearance, sometimes called the fuselage or projectile look.

Designers offered a fastback for the 1962 model, but it did not go into production. A radical wedge theme was considered for the 1980 model, but Ford executive Lee Iacocca wanted a more conservative look.

Thunderbird offered three models in 1967.

CHAPTER 8

BIG 'BIRDS

The early Thunderbirds were small, sleek and beautiful, but many drivers wanted more room. The 1958 model gave it to them. For the first time, buyers could choose a four-seater model.

The *squarebird*, as it is sometimes called, provided interior room and comfort equal to full-sized sedans, but the car sat 10 inches lower to the ground. The 1958 T-Bird was the first with a body built as a single unit.

Ford spent $40 million re-engineering the Thunderbird for 1958. An upright, formal roof line and longer doors (more than 4 feet) allowed ease of entry and exit. A convertible top that could flip backward into the trunk was an option. The engine was a V-8 rated at 300 bhp.

With the 1958 model, Thunderbird became more of a family luxury car than a sports car.

The lines of this 1959 convertible illustrate why the Thunderbirds of the time were called "squarebirds."

	1958 Fairlane	1958 Thunderbird
	(measurements given in inches)	
Length	207.2	205.4
Width	78	77
Height	56.2	52.5
Wheelbase	118	113
Ground clearance	6	5.8
Front legroom	43.2	43.4
Rear legroom	40.8	38.8

In many ways, the 1958 squarebird resembled the 1958 Ford Fairlane, a large, low-to-the-ground family car. Ford Motor Company had, with its redesign, made the Thunderbird into a luxury limousine with a sporty feel about it. Because of its new size and style, the T-Bird could no longer be called a sports car.

The new four-seater model became popular and sold well for the next several years. In fact, the 1960 sales would remain a high point for Thunderbird sales for 16 years to come.

The 1960 T-Bird had the classic roof line and a distinctive oval grille.

The 1959 T-Bird scored a big win at the new Daytona 500, a 500-mile contest for stock cars, raced on a 2.5-mile tri-oval speedway.

CHAPTER 9

MOST POPULAR 'BIRDS

In terms of numbers sold, the newly designed 1977 model swept the market. "It has a taut, linear shape," reported *Car and Driver* magazine, "with the sort of bold styling gestures usually seen only on show cars."

Standard equipment on the '77 T-Bird included the 302 cubic inch V-8 engine, which produced 130 bhp. However, buyers could choose the optional 173-bhp, 400-cubic-incher. A shorter wheelbase meant the '77 handled better than any T-Bird before it.

The styling crew chose a unique new combination for the car. A lean lower body was combined with a slim-line roof. The most outstanding feature was the new door-pillar and window design. The 1977, '78 and '79 models are easily recognizable today as a result of this unique design.

The '77 weighed 630 pounds less than the previous model. It flew from 0 to 60 mph in 11.5 seconds. And it made the quarter-mile in just 17.9 seconds, the best T-Bird performance in years.

Another design feature helped make the sales of Thunderbird shoot up during the 1977 to 1979 model years. The wheelbase was reduced to 114 inches – a match with other Ford models. Since the T-Bird could be built on a mass-market chassis, Ford could sell it at a much lower price. The $5,063 base price was an amazing 35 percent reduction. For the first time, large numbers of people could afford a new Thunderbird.

Year	Sales
1955	14,771
1965	68,663
1976	46,713
1977	**300,066**
1978	**319,328**
1979	**219,465**
1980	164,795
1981	80,942
1982	47,903
Total sold from 1955-89:	3,294,391

The 1977 Thunderbird was
so popular that people
bought almost seven times
more than were sold in 1966.

The 1979 model featured
hidden headlights.

CHAPTER 10

TREND SETTER

The interior console between bucket seats, shown here from a 1992 T-Bird, was a concept first developed by Thunderbird designers.

Many features that are now standard on automobiles worldwide first appeared on the Ford Thunderbird. It was the T-Bird that first came out with a button on the automatic gear-shift lever that must be depressed before it can be shifted past neutral. This lockout device prevents transmission damage from accidental shifting.

A dramatic innovation developed by T-Bird designers was the center console between the bucket seats in the '58 model – a device still used in most cars with bucket seats.

Designers solved a problem with the console. The problem was that the low body style of the 1958 model left passengers sitting in a tunnel. To keep the roof line low, riders had to sit in a channel between the high drive train and the high doorsills. The full-length center console, combined with the split dashboard style, gave the 1958 and later T-Birds a dual cockpit appearance copied by sports cars for years to come.

Thunderbird also introduced the door-ajar warning light and power door locks. Some people thought such extras were silly gimmicks when they first appeared in 1964. Today, they are standard equipment on most cars. The '64 T-Birds also sported flow-through ventilation.

Newer safety design features include a fuel tank tucked ahead of the rear axle so that it is not punctured in an auto crash. Also for safety, the drive shaft is designed to collapse like a telescope on impact.

The 1978 Sports option T-Bird looked and drove like a mid-sized luxury car.

CHAPTER 11

WINNING 'BIRDS

Three times, the Thunderbird has earned the coveted *Motor Trend* Car of the Year Award.

The editors of *Motor Trend* magazine test drive new models each year. They choose a car that is exceptional in performance and design.

After years of looking boxy, Thunderbird acquired sleek, rounded lines in '87, winning its second Car of the Year award.

The 1958 model was the first Thunderbird to earn the award: it gained praise from the magazine staff for its "totally new concept in interior packaging." The editors also wrote that "the ride of the new Thunderbird is as comfortable as any American car today, regardless of size."

This luxurious 1958 model was the first T-Bird with four seats instead of two. Ford officials argued whether a four-seater would sell as well as the smaller, two-seat models. They questioned T-Bird owners. The majority thought a back seat would be an improvement. They were right. Sales of Thunderbirds increased after a back seat was added to the design.

The second of Thunderbird's Car of the Year Awards was presented to the 1987 model. It had a whole new look that cost Ford $250 million to create. Every body panel except the hood and fenders had been changed.

On December 26, 1988, the model that was to become the third T-Bird to be named Car of the Year was unveiled. *Motor Trend* editors called the 1988 Thunderbird "one of the most balanced and controllable cars we've ever driven."

When Thunderbird grew from the sporty, small car of the first T-Birds into the 1958 squarebird, Motor Trend *magazine named it Car of the Year.*

The 1988 Thunderbird was also named Car of the Year by Motor Trend *magazine.*

CHAPTER 12

HIGH-TECH 'BIRDS

Through the years Thunderbird has remained on the cutting edge of performance technology. Among the high-tech equipment features on recent 'Birds are:

- An anti-lock brake system (ABS) – each wheel is monitored by a computer. When the driver hits the brakes hard, the computer automatically applies and releases the brakes rapidly, up to 10 times per second! This prevents wheel lock up and stops spinning out of control.

- Speed-sensitive steering – a computer senses and automatically adjusts the amount of power steering needed for each driving condition. During tight, low-speed maneuvers such as parallel parking, steering is easy. As speed increases, steering is more firm for better control.

- Automatic suspension – most sports cars have a rough ride. New Thunderbirds, though, have an automatic suspension system. It's controlled by a microprocessor that monitors the speed, brake pressure, acceleration and steering conditions. Usually, the shocks absorb most bounce so that the ride will be smooth. On tight curves or at high speeds, the shocks ease up so that the driver will have more control.

- A traction-lok axle – when roads have ice, snow or mud on them, the traction-lok axle automatically shifts some of the driving force, or torque, to the wheel with the most traction. This feature helps prevent skidding and getting stuck.

The dash of the 1993 Thunderbird displays tachometer and supercharger booster gauges, temperature and oil pressure gauges in easy-to-see white on a black background.

With the anti-lock brake system (ABS), drivers can brake hard on slick surfaces without fishtailing around.

One option on the 1993 Thunderbird is a remote-controlled door lock system.

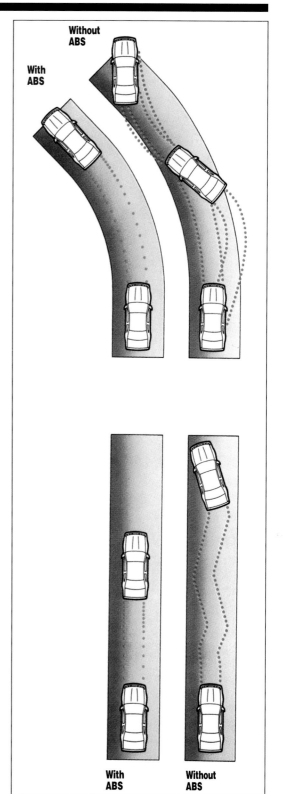

CHAPTER 13

WHAT MAKES 'BIRDS FLY?

The "HO" stamped on Thunderbird's 5.0 liter V-8 engine stands for "high output."

Drivers who choose a Thunderbird can also choose the type of engine they prefer.

- The traditional V-8 is the favorite choice of many T-Bird drivers. This big engine is 5.0 liters in size. With sequential electronic fuel injection (EFI), the driver gets more miles to the gallon of gasoline.

  The V-8 engine produces 200 horsepower (hp) at 4000 revolutions per minute (rpm). And it delivers 275 pound feet of torque at 3000 rpm.

- Thunderbird's standard engine is the 3.8 liter V-6. It also has sequential electronic fuel injection.

- The supercharged, modified 3.8 V-6 delivers greater horsepower and torque by increasing the pressure of the intake charge. Drivers experience rapid acceleration similar to that delivered by bigger V-8 engines.

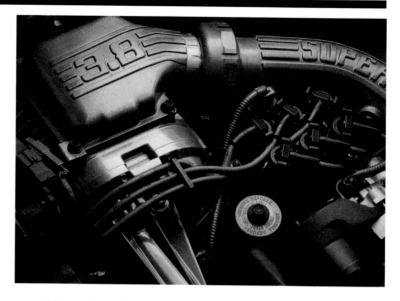

How does the supercharger work? A supercharger uses an air pump that sends bigger blasts of fuel and air to the cylinders. A more powerful combustion stroke creates more power and more speed.

Thunderbird also uses an intercooler located between the supercharger and the combustion chamber. The intercooler lowers the temperature of the air passing through it. Cooler air can be packed together more densely in the engine. More air in the engine means more oxygen for burning fuel, which means greater horsepower.

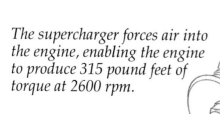

The supercharger forces air into the engine, enabling the engine to produce 315 pound feet of torque at 2600 rpm.

CHAPTER 14

THUNDERBIRD: IMPORTANT DATES

1951 Ford executive Lewis Crusoe attended the Paris Auto Salon. Inspired by European sports cars, he wanted Ford designers to make an American model.

1952 Design Director Franklin Hershey heard from a friend that Chevrolet was working on a sports car design – the Corvette. He began making clay models and drawings of what would become the Ford Thunderbird.

1954 February, a prototype Ford sports car was presented at the Detroit Auto Show as a wooden mock-up; it did not yet have a name.

1954 October, the completed Thunderbird was presented to the public for purchase at the base price of $2,695.

1958 Thunderbird received *Motor Trend*'s Car of the Year Award. Known as the "squarebird," this model was a four-seater – bigger, faster and more plush than earlier 'Birds.

1961 The "projectile" look appeared with a dual cockpit dash panel and swing-away steering wheel.

1972 The one-millionth Thunderbird rolled off the assembly line. A Landau model, it was purchased by a California collector.

1976 The last of the "big 'Birds" was produced. A commemorative model featured a spare-tire bulge in the trunk lid, a vinyl half-roof and a moon roof.

1978 Ford sold more Thunderbirds than ever before or since.

1983 Sleek, new aerodynamic styling appeared; features included rounded contours, sloping hood, sharply raked windshield and back light, and wrap-over doors with concealed drip moldings.

1987 The high-performance Turbo Coupe earned Thunderbird its second Car of the Year Award. Features included an intercooler and dual exhausts boosting horsepower to 190 (with manual transmission).

1988 For a third time, Thunderbird was honored with the Car of the Year Award. A race-prepared Thunderbird carried Bill Elliott to the NASCAR Winston Cup Championship.

1990 Thunderbird celebrated its 35th anniversary with a limited-edition model Super Coupe. Artistic cloisonné emblems disintegrate if removed, to prevent their being mounted on another model.

Today and into the future – Thunderbird continues to please drivers with its styling, comfort and performance. Designers at Ford Motor Company promise a continuation of their past record for innovation in comfort, style and safety. The Thunderbird will make increasing use of computer chips for performance and driver safety.

GLOSSARY

bhp – Brake horsepower; a measurement of engine power by using a braking device to determine the amount of power an engine has at high revolutions per minute (rpm).

carburetor – The device used in gasoline engines to produce an explosive vapor of fuel and air.

chassis (CHAS-ee) – The rectangular frame attached to the axles that supports the body and motor of a car.

coupe – A car with two doors.

cylinder – In an engine, the chamber in which the piston moves.

Fairlane – A large family car made by Ford Motor Company.

torque – Turning force, a measure of engine power at low rpm.

hp – Horsepower; a measurement of engine power.

mph – Miles per hour.

prototype – An original form that serves as a model on which later models are based.

rpm – Revolutions per minute; a measurement of how rapidly an engine turns.

sedan – A four-door car.

stock car – A car of standard make that has been modified for racing.

turbocharger – A device that uses the exhaust gas of the engine to drive a turbine that in turn drives a supercharger attached to the engine.

INDEX